Integrating European Financial Services:

A Grounded Theory Approach

Kerry E Howell

Discussion Paper Series

This Discussion Paper Series is issued by the Ashcroft International Business School. All papers submitted are subject to a refereeing process and the views expressed are those of the author and not necessarily those of the Business School. The papers often represent preliminary or developing work, which is circulated to facilitate discussion and comment.

Aims of the Series

❏ Promote the dissemination of Business School research within the institution and through the wider research community;

❏ Further promote the research profile and ethos of the Business School;

❏ Promote a greater awareness of the wide range of research specialisms within the Business School, leading to a cross-fertilisation of ideas and greater evolution of team research;

❏ Provide a mechanism for the discussion, review and development of research ideas.

Editors of Discussion Paper Series

Dr Kerry Howell, Professor Peter Woolliams, Dr Paul Saw
Ashcroft International Business School

For further information about this and other Discussion Papers in the series, please contact:

Dr Kerry E. Howell
Ashcroft International Business School
Anglia Polytechnic University
Victoria Road South
Chelmsford, Essex
CM1 1LL
United Kingdom

Tel: +44 (0)1245 493131
Fax: +44 (0)1245 348768
Email: k.e.howell@apu.ac.uk

Author profile

Dr Howell is a Reader and Jean Monnet Associate in the Ashcroft International Business School at Anglia Polytechnic University (APU) and undertakes teaching in European integration, policy-making and governance, business regulation and European business. He has published widely in academic journals and has recently written a book on European integration and financial services. Dr Howell has acted as a consultant for Cambridge Econometrics, the European Capital Market Institute as well as numerous financial services companies and interest groups. He is presently undertaking research in areas relating to European governance, ethical issues in corporate governance, capital market regulation and constitutional change.

Address for correspondence:
Dr Kerry E. Howell
Ashcroft International Business School
Anglia Polytechnic University
Victoria Road South
Chelmsford, Essex
CM1 1LL
United Kingdom

Tel: +44 (0)1245 493131
Fax: +44 (0)1245 348768
Email: k.e.howell@apu.ac.uk

First published October 2002

Chlorine free paper

ISBN 1-900-432-41-2

Published by:

PUBLICATIONS LIMITED

Linda Golding
Earlybrave Publications Limited
Springfield Lyons House
Chelmsford Business Park
Chelmsford
Essex CM2 5TH
United Kingdom

Tel: +44 (0)1245 236506
Fax: +44 (0)1245 236611
Email: lgolding@earlybrave.com

Further copies available from the publisher.

Earlybrave Publications Limited is part of the Clifford Thames Group of companies.

Printed in the United Kingdom by The Printing Place Ltd.

Abstract

This paper examines a methodological technique (grounded theory) and illustrates how it is applied in a study of European Integration. The methodology is provided through categorisation and process, in conjunction with theoretical coding (open, axial and selective) and the construction of a substantive theory that attempts to further our understanding of both meta theory e.g. historical institutionalism and multi level governance and grand or formal theories of European integration e.g. neo-functionalism and intergovernmentalism.

In the aftermath of the Single European Act (SEA), the beginnings of the Single European Market (SEM), the Maastricht Treaty and Economic and Monetary Union (EMU) it became evident that industries/sectors needed to involve themselves in the creation of the European Union. This paper illustrates the extent of industry/sector involvement through developing a substantive theory, which investigates and clarifies a number of theoretical propositions relating to the formal theories. Overall, the paper provides a study of how meta and substantive theories may better explain European integration processes.

Introduction

The aim of this paper is to illustrate an application of grounded theory in the context of European integration. Following a discussion of European integration theory the paper undertakes a comparative analysis of Member State life insurance legislation and through induction, deduction and verification formulates a matrix and model to illustrate policy-making processes in European Union (EU) institutions. The paper argues that theory can be normative, meta substantive and formal or grand and develops a substantive theory to illustrate its relationship with existing meta and formal theories. Substantive theory emerges from the analysis of a " . . . particular situational context", whereas meta and formal theory " . . . emerge from a study of phenomenon under many different types of situations" (Corbin and Strauss, 1990; p 174). The difference is the scope of the attempted explanation. Normative theory deals with what ought to be rather than what is and in the political context finds expression in moral perspectives on institutions and policies in abstract and practical terms (Glaser, 1995). Of course, substantive, meta and formal theory will all carry normative perspectives.

From a positivist perspective, theory should have shared assumptions and predict or make generalisations about outcomes. However, the extent that theory should generalise or predict are serious bones of contention not only in the context of European integration but social science in general. One may argue that most prediction in social sciences are generalisations or trends. This illustrates a shift from the naïve and critical realism ontologies proposed by positivism and post-positivism[1] to the historical realism identified by critical theory. Glaser and Strauss (1967) and Strauss and Corbin (1990) build on the idea of historical realism and argue that theory can never be complete but is historically developed and through data collection, re-analysis and re-interpretation transforms and evolves.

Initially, the paper discusses substantive meta and formal theories of European integration. Second, it discusses grounded theory and explains how it is applied to European integration. Third, the means of data collection are briefly overviewed and the grounded theory mode of analysis made explicit. Finally, the paper provides a substantive theory based on the research findings and reassesses the meta and formal theories.

Substantive and Formal Theory

Glaser and Strauss (1967) argued that grounded theory was concerned with two types of theory: substantive and formal. They emphasised that theory generation was accomplished through the collection, coding and analysis of data and that these three operations, as far as was possible, were undertaken together. Collection, coding and analysis should interact throughout the investigation their separation hinders theory generation and set ideas stifle it. This study generates a substantive theory in relation to formal theories e.g. neo-functionalism and intergovernmentalism and investigates them regarding their applicability as theories of European integration. Substantive theory necessitates four central criteria.

Fit, comprehension, generality and *control*: First, theory should be induced from diverse data and be faithful to reality (it should fit). Secondly, the *fit* should be comprehensible; thirdly, the data should be comprehensive and interpretations conceptually wide (there should be *generality*). Finally, in relation to generality, it should be made clear when conditions apply to specific situations and phenomenon (there should be *control*) (Corbin and Strauss, 1990).

---

[1] Positivism and post-positivism are paradigms of inquiry. Positivism considers that an apprehensible reality exists through which immutable and natural laws may be derived. Post-positivism also considers that reality exists but it argues that because of the human condition (the flawed human intellect) it cannot be understood perfectly. Consequently, reality must be subjected to wide critical examination so it can be understood as near as possible (but never perfectly). Of course, definitions of theory are different when understood from a critical theory or constructivist perspective (see Guba and Lincoln, 1994).

Neo-functionalism proposes that the EU is a supranational entity, which through its growing authority encourages the transferral of allegiance away from national institutions toward the European. On the other hand, intergovernmentalism argues that the nation-state is the main impetus behind European integration. At a fundamental level neo-functionalism may be considered an incremental process, which argues that through the transfer of allegiance to a supranational body, the use of interest groups and the concept of spillover European integration is intensified[2]. Intergovernmentalism, on the other hand, identifies the nation-state as the primary impetus behind the European integration process.

In this context, one may question whether intergovernmentalism and neo-functionalism may be labelled formal theories. Neither has emerged from studies under different types of situations i.e. integration processes external to Western Europe.

On the other hand, neo-functionalism and intergovernmentalism could be seen as formal theories in relation to multi-level governance, state-centricism and historical institutionalism and these could be identified as formal theories in relation to this study. Or they could be seen as substantive theories that are " . . . generated from the data . . . in order to see which of diverse formal theories are, perhaps, applicable for furthering additional substantive formulations" (Glaser and Strauss, 1967; p 34).

The interaction between formal and substantive theory may be observed in the way the EU " . . . has . . . been studied as an example of . . . supranational integration or intergovernmental co-operation between, (previously) sovereign nation-states" (Hix, 1994; p 1). (For further discussion see Haas, 1958; 1964; George, 1994; 1995; Keohane and Hoffman, 1990; 1991; Lindberg, 1963; Morganthau, 1973; Moravcsik, 1991; 1993; Mutimer, 1989; Sandholtz and Zysman 1989; Sandholtz 1994; Trakholme-Mikkelson, 1991). Some theorists have attempted to refine intergovernmentalism in their development of substantive theory (Moravscik, 1993, 1995) while others have drawn on aspects of both neo-functionalism and intergovernmentalism (Keohane and Hoffman, 1991 Sandholtz 1993, 1996; Sbaragia 1993b; Marks, 1993; Marks, 1995 Marks et al 1996 and Marks et al, 1996a; Pierson 1996; Hooghie and Marks 1997; Sandholtz and Stone

---

[2] Spillover is what Haas (1958) labelled the " . . . expansive logic of sector integration" (p 243). The expansive logic of sector integration through a variety of sectors swapping concessions indicated the motor of political integration (ibid). Haas also described spillover as " . . . the accretion of new powers and tasks to a central institutional structure, based on changing demands and the expectation on the part of such political actors as interest groups, political parties and bureaucracies" (Haas, cited in Kirchner, 1976; p 3).

Sweet 1998). In addition, there are a number of studies relating to the practicalities of EU policy-making, through the study of specific sub-national interests and their interactions with EU policy-making institutions, which again may be interpreted as substantive theories. (See Camerra-Rowe, 1996; Coen, 1997; 1998; Greenwood et al, 1992; Greenwood and Cram, 1996; Greenwood, 1995; 1997; Howell, 1999, 2000; Mazey and Richardson, 1996; McLaughlin et al, 1993; McLaughlin and Greenwood, 1995; McLaughlin, 1995; Sandholtz and Stone Sweet, 1998). Indeed such studies provide substantive theories against which the formal theories may be measured.

Hooghe and Marks (1997) link neo-functionalism (through supranational actors and interest groups) to multi-level governance and intergovernmentalism to state-centric governance. They conclude that intergovernmentalism is not able to fully explain European policy-making processes; that policy-making is of a multi-level nature. Indeed, Marks et al (1996) provide an interesting interpretation of the present situation. "Multi-level governance does not confront the sovereignty of states directly. Instead of being explicitly challenged states in the European Union are being melded gently into multi-level polity by their leaders and the actions of numerous sub-national and supranational actors. State-centric theorists are right when they argue that states are extremely powerful institutions that are capable of crushing direct threats to their existence" (p 371). Pierson (1996) lays the foundations of a criticism of intergovernmentalism from a historical institutionalist perspective. Historical institutionalism is a broad perspective but it does encompass two unifying themes. It " . . . is historical because it recognises that political development must be understood as a process that unfolds over time. It is institutionalist because it stresses that many of the contemporary implications of these temporal processes are embedded in institutions – whether these are formal rules, policy structures, or norms" (p 126) (for further on historical institutionalism see Bulmer, 1994; 1997; 2000; Guy Peters, 2001; Hall and Taylor, 1996; March and Olsen, 1999).

As noted, each of these theoretical perspectives draw on more abstract levels of theory and are substantive and formal in relation to one another. For instance, historical institutionalism and multi-level governance may be identified as substantive theories in relation to neo-functional and intergovernmental theories. Indeed, there is a hierarchy of theory based on abstraction and extent of generalisation. The substantive theory developed in this study is limited in terms of both abstraction and extent of generalisation and at the bottom of this hierarchy. Indeed, it could be seen as a substantive theory in relation to historical institutionalism and multi-level governance. Overall, neo-functionalism and intergovernmentalism may be seen as formal or general theories, historical institutionalism and multi-level governance as meta-theories, and this study as the basis of a substantive theory.

An Application of Grounded Theory

Grounded theory involves the " . . . soliciting of emic viewpoints to assist in determining the meaning and purposes that people ascribe to their actions" (Guba and Lincoln, 1994; p 110). "Grounded theory methodology incorporates . . . assumption(s) . . . concerning the human status of actors whom we study. They have perspectives on and interpretations of their own and other actors' actions. As researchers we are required to learn what we can of their interpretations and perspectives" (Strauss and Corbin, 1994; p 280 author's brackets). This study considers that this is the basis of grounded theory: an attempt to understand reality through social constructions and an attempt at objectivity through recognising the subjectivity of the researcher and researched in terms of their interpretative nature.

Grounded theory wishes to demote the idea that the discovery of relevant concepts and hypotheses are a *priori* to research (Glaser and Strauss, 1967; Glaser, 1978; Charmaz, 1983; Strauss, 1987; Strauss and Corbin, 1990; Corbin and Strauss, 1990; Glaser, 1992; Strauss and Corbin, 1994). Grounded theory posits that theory is derived from data and cannot be divorced from the developmental process. In general this means that hypotheses and concepts are generated and interpreted in relation to the data throughout the research (Glaser and Strauss, 1967; Charmaz, 1983).

In general terms, " . . . (a)nalysis makes use of constant comparisons. As incidents are noted, they should be continually compared against other incidents for dissimilarities and likeness" (Corbin and Strauss, 1990; p 9). This study compares Member State life insurance legislation to identify the extent of free trade in the national life insurance markets. This is a standard means of generating theory and is usually accomplished early in the study to put the "story straight" (Glaser and Strauss, 1967; Strauss and Corbin, 1990; pp 116-142; Oyen 1990). "Making comparisons assists the researcher in guarding against bias . . . comparisons also help to achieve greater precision (the grouping of like and only like phenomenon)"

(Corbin and Strauss, 1990; p 9). Indeed, one is seeking regularities this also creates order and helps with data integration.

Data Sampling

Data sampling was based on the grounded theory technique of *theoretical sampling*. *Theoretical sampling* is undertaken on the basis that ". . . concepts have proven *theoretical relevance* to the evolving theory" (Strauss and Corbin, 1990; p 176). *Theoretical sampling* involves three processes: *open sampling* which relates to *open coding; relational and variational sampling* which is associated with *axial coding*; and *discriminate sampling* which is linked to *selective coding* (coding processes are discussed pp12-22). *Proven theoretical relevance* identifies concepts that are significant enough to be considered *categories* " . . . they are deemed significant because (1) they are repeatedly present or notably absent when comparing incident after incident (2) through coding procedures they earn the status of categories. . . . The aim of theoretical sampling is to sample events, incidents, and so forth, that are indicative of categories, their properties and dimensions, so that you can develop and conceptually relate them" (ibid, p 177).

Survey A:	Survey of European Union life insurance companies. Allows an understanding of market environment perceptions from separate Member States. Open sampling and relational and variational sampling.
Survey B:	Survey of UK insurance companies to ascertain interest group utilisation. Discriminate sampling.
Interviews:	The interviews are supplemented by Survey B and provide an in-depth understanding of the EU policy-making process with regard to the Third Life Assurance Directive. Relational and variational sampling and discriminate sampling.
Observations and preliminary discussions:	
	This incorporated three months in Brussels working with a European political consultant (GJW), a period with the European section of a UK company (Commercial Union) open discussions and close contact with the Association of British Insurers (ABI). Open sampling.

Table One: Data Collection Scheme

Following an inductive analysis of the different Member States' life insurance legislation and a survey (see p15) of the European life insurance industry, a regulatory environment matrix was created. This part of the of the analysis illustrates *open sampling* where the aim is ". . . to uncover as many potentially relevant categories as possible along with their properties and dimensions" (ibid, p 181) and the beginnings of *relational* and *variational sampling*. Indeed, Survey A validates the relationships between the categories and identifies processes. From this some propositions were formed and the sampling gradually became specifically *relational* and *variational* (see Table One).

The sampling was undertaken purposefully which encompassed choosing individuals and documentation that demonstrated variations in the categories and what happened when change occurred. As with the coding (see pp 12-22) the distinction between relational and variational sampling and discriminate sampling became unclear. *Discriminate sampling* is direct and deliberate and is indicated in the choice of interviewees and Survey B (see Table One). "In discriminate sampling, a researcher chooses the sites, persons and documents that will maximise opportunities for verifying the story line and relationships between categories" (ibid, p 187). Sampling in grounded theory studies is concerned with the " . . . representativeness of concepts in their varying forms. In each instance of data collection, we look for evidence of its significant presence or absence, and ask why?" (ibid, p 190) (see Table One). Grounded theory studies look " . . . for incidents and events that are indicative of phenomena" (ibid). They pursue density and " . . . the more interviews, observations and documents obtained, then the more evidence will accumulate, the more variations will be found, and the greater the density will be achieved. Thus there will be wider applicability of the theory, because more and different sets of conditions affecting phenomena are uncovered" (ibid pp 190-91).

Theoretical Coding
Theoretical coding is linked closely to the theoretical sampling and encompasses the very basis of grounded theory. The essential relationship between data and theory is a conceptual code. The code conceptualises the underlying patterns of the data. "Thus, in generating a theory by developing the hypothetical relationships between conceptual codes (categories and their properties) which have been generated from the data as indicators, we discover a grounded theory" (Glaser, 1978; p 55). There are three types of theoretical coding; open, axial and selective.

Open Coding
Open coding is closely linked to open sampling and provides the foundation of the research process. "The goal of the analyst is to generate an emergent set of

categories and their properties which fit, work and are relevant for integrating theory. To achieve this goal the analyst begins with open coding" (Glaser, 1978; p 56). To accomplish open coding in this study the qualitative data relating to each regulatory environment was broken down and restructured initially on a table and later refined in a matrix. The *category* of 'Regulatory Environment' emerged following an analysis of Member State legislation and regulations (see Table Two). Through further research *conceptual labels* emerged in terms of liberal, prescribed and state-controlled regulatory environments and each of these was made up of the *properties* outlined (see Table Two). A *category* is a " . . . classification of concepts. This classification is discovered when concepts are compared one against another and appear to pertain to a similar phenomenon (Corbin and Strauss, 1990; p 61). Furthermore, *conceptual labels* are placed " . . . on discrete happenings, events, and other instances of phenomena" (ibid). Indeed, these concepts are made up of *properties* and *characteristics* that are indicated by the overall category. Finally, the Member States are given *dimensions* through the " . . . location of properties along a continuum" (ibid, p 197), in this research a regulation table and matrix.

This process was pursued through the use of *code, theoretical, operational notes* and *diagrams*. *Code notes* illustrate separate types of legislation in the different Member States and how aspects of the legislation link together and fluctuate under *conceptual labels*. *Theoretical notes* link different types of cultural existence to the conceptual labels and investigates how compromise takes place, whereas, the *operational notes* illustrated the need for further research. The *operational notes* guided the research in respect of; whom to survey; the questions to be asked, who should be interviewed and the structure the interviews should take. Overall, the research was visually represented through *diagrams*, which illustrated the relationship between *concepts*. Indeed, the *diagrams* illustrate a " . . . visual sorting process that helps you identify how the categories are related to one another" (ibid).

Open coding was used to create a scale of one to twelve on which a totally liberal regulatory environment is valued one and a completely state-controlled or nationalised regulatory environment is valued twelve. A prescribed regulatory environment is not one of primarily self-regulation, nor is it completely state-controlled: it is a market with tight government controls (see Majone, 1994 for further). The higher the number on the matrix the greater the regulation and state-control indicated in the Member State's legislative system. Through further comparative analysis and open coding each Member State was understood to be at some point on the matrix scale (see Table Two and Life Insurance Regulation Matrix One, Figure One).

Regulatory Environments (CATEGORY)	Legislative/Regulatory Stipulations	Member States
Liberal (CONCEPTUAL LABEL)	(PROPERTIES)	(DIMENSION-ALISATION)
1	Completely free market Approval of Company	
2 - 3	Solvency Margins Policyholder protection Evaluation of Liability & Rates	Luxembourg Netherlands UK
3 - 4	Open Access to Insurance Information	Republic of Ireland
Prescribed 5 - 6 Marketing Controls 7 - 8	Price Controls Denmark Solvency Deposit Policy Approval Regulation of Contract	Belgium Spain Germany
State-Controlled 9 - 10 10 - 11 12	State Controlled Companies Contractual Obligation to State Intense Monitoring of Companies Proof of Ability Total State Control	France Italy Portugal Greece

Table Two: Regulatory/ Legislative Environment Table

Once this had been achieved further investigation and verification were necessary and a survey of the European life insurance sector was undertaken (Survey A). In Survey A, three hundred questionnaires were sent to insurance companies in eight of twelve Member States, (the UK, Germany, France, Italy, Belgium, Netherlands, Spain and Republic of Ireland). Four Member States were omitted mainly because of problems with translation and difficulties in terms of acquiring addresses. The response rate was 35%. Survey A wished to illustrate the thoughts of the Member States regarding Member State life insurance regulation and the creation of a SEM. It also aimed to determine the extent of liberality allowed within a particular Member State, illustrate what the respondents considered to be the optimum regulation for trading and the amount of legislation necessary to enable this. Fundamentally, it acted as a means of verifying the initial open coding.

Survey A. A Survey of the European Life Insurance Industry
(1)   How liberal or state controlled is your national life insurance market?
(2)   Where would you place the Single European Market (SEM) life insurance sector in respect of regulatory freedom?
(3)   What type of regulatory environment do you consider that the SEM should be to allow your company its greatest advantage?
(4)   What type of regulatory environment do you consider the SEM in life insurance should be to allow the greatest consumer protection?
(5)   What type of regulatory environment do you consider the SEM in life insurance should be to allow the greatest consumer choice?

Survey A was used instead of interviews, because a broad sample was required to add to and verify the regulatory environment matrix which encompassed the industry's understanding of the SEM and the EU. Indeed, the survey provided an understanding of the differences in Member State normative thinking in respect of life insurance regulation and raised the question of where and how compromise takes place in the creation of the SEM.

1-2	=	self-minimal regulation
3-4	=	minimal regulation; independent regulatory bodies
5-6	=	moderately regulated without state ownership
7-8	=	highly regulated without state ownership
9-10	=	highly regulated with minimal state ownership
11-12	=	highly regulated with a profusion of state control.

Table Three: Regulation Scale

The matrix was subsequently revised taking into consideration the survey results, which also raised further questions (See Life Insurance Regulation Matrix Two, Figure Two). Question one of Survey A allowed a revision of the level of Member State regulation (as noted in Regulation Matrix One) and question three provided a generalisation regarding compromise. This was identified as falling between 4.5 and 6.5 on Regulation Matrix Two. Consequently, the Third Life Assurance Directive should have been identified between these levels with the Compromise Convergence Point materialising once mutual recognition had come into play.

Liberal			Prescribed				Nationalised				
1	2	3	4	5	6	7	8	9	10	11	12
Luxemburg											
UK											
Netherlands											
Republic of Ireland											
Belgium											
Denmark											
Germany											
Spain											
Italy											
France											
Portugal											
Greece											
CCP											

CCP = Compromised Convergence Point
Matrix compiled from an analysis of Munich Re. (1988), Financial Times (1992), Sigma Re. (1988-93), Pool (1991), BIIC and CEA Working Papers.

Figure One: Life Insurance Regulation Matrix One

The matrices subsequently set up a number of questions, which were investigated through semi-structured interviews with key individuals in the creation of the Third Life Assurance Directive, and through observations of the European policy-making process. For instance, even though Survey A identified that compromise was possible how this may be achieved was uncertain. The research needed an understanding of the policy-making process, the interviews enabled this and provided further development of a substantive theory. (See Table One for a summary of the data collection process in terms of three surveys, the interviews and observations.)

Formulating and Coding Semi-Structured Interview Questions
Grounded theory entails two basic analytical procedures. Firstly, one continually makes comparisons and secondly one asks questions. As noted above, these processes have been adhered to in earlier parts of the study. However, at this point

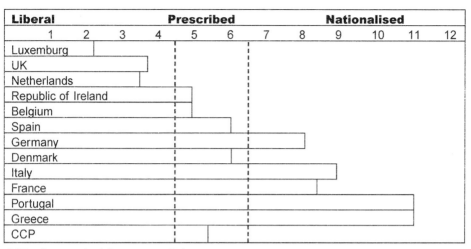

Liberal				Prescribed				Nationalised			
1	2	3	4	5	6	7	8	9	10	11	12
Luxemburg											
UK											
Netherlands											
Republic of Ireland											
Belgium											
Spain											
Germany											
Denmark											
Italy											
France											
Portugal											
Greece											
CCP											

CCP = Compromised Convergence Point
Matrix compiled from an analysis of Munich Re. (1988), Financial Times (1992), Sigma Re. (1988-93), Pool (1991), BIIC and CEA Working Papers and survey of EU life insurance industry.

Figure Two: Life Insurance Regulation Matrix Two

the study wishes to explain the process in relation to the interviews. Questioning opens up the data and the categories properties and dimensions constructed earlier in the study allowed the researcher to ask questions more precisely in the interviews. There are general questions that can be drawn from the data, which can stimulate a series of questions, which in turn " . . . lead to the development of further categories, properties and dimensions. The basic questions are *"Who? When? Where? What? How? And How Much?"* (Strauss and Corbin, 1990; p 77). The interview questions build on the basic questions and the previous categories that were generated in the initial open coding. Indeed, the difficulties that were created through the categorisation of the European life insurance industry provide the basis and strategy of the interview questions. *How* can compromise be realised? *How much* compromise between the different interpretations (Liberal, Prescribed, State-Controlled) can be realised? *When* and *Where* is compromise realised? The basis of the interviews is European integration and from this five other categories emerge: Understanding, Negotiation, Interaction, Difference and Compromise. They emerge through data collection and analysis and deal with the problems the study uncovered.

The interviews were conducted on a semi-formal basis and centred around 12 core questions these were:
(1) What are the major functions of the CEA/BIPAR/ABI/the Commission/the Council/National Supervisors and how do these fit with each other at:
    (A) The EU level
    (B) The national level?
(2) To what extent are decisions made with interest group/COREPER/ Commission/National Supervisor in-put?
(3) Who defines decision parameters is it interest groups, national supervisors, the Council of Ministers or the Commission?
(4) Does the Council, the Commission, national legislatures and interest groups reach a compromise prior to a decision reaching the Council?
(5) Does an interaction exist between the Council / the Commission / national supervisors and specific interest groups at a national and European level?
(6) How does the Council/national supervisor know what to insist upon in respect of national interest?
(7) How much interaction exists between interest groups / Commission/ Council / national supervisor and the Insurance Committee?
(8) Were different Member States looking for specific types of life insurance regulatory environments for the SEM which is different from other member states?
(9) Were there differences between the:
    (a) The French ideal
    (b) The German ideal
    (c) The Dutch ideal
    (d) The UK ideal
    (e) The Italian ideal
    Please illustrate these differences.
    How does your market ideal fit into these?
(10) How are compromises reached between the different national interest groups prior to the Commission initially drawing up draft legislation? Is

there an interaction between the interest group at the European level and the Commission which takes into consideration a compromise reached by the member state interest groups i.e. ABI through membership of the European interest group CEA/BIPAR.

(11) *Where/When possible have compromises been reached between the Council, the Commission and Parliament before the final negotiations to enable a more efficient means of decision making?*

(12) *What takes precedence in the formulation of a Directive Member State or industry/sector interests?*

The questions were coded so the same could be asked of each interviewee. This allowed the five categories to emerge from the interviews (for further, see p20 interview results). As noted, the interviews identified the emergence of five categories, each built around the core category of European integration.

Interviews were used to investigate policy-making processes at the European level. Over a ten-week period working for a political lobbyist company in Brussels, the author was able to observe the policy-making process. Interviews were undertaken with the Commission, insurance interest groups, the UK Permanent Representative and lobbyists. Further interviews were undertaken in Paris and the UK.

Each interview attempted to look at the same phenomenon from a different perspective and enable data 'saturation'. The interviews were conducted between Surveys A and B and indicated the need for Survey B (see Data Collection Scheme and theoretical sampling). The open coding process, the surveys and subsequent matrices indicated the need for legislative convergence. Additionally, the interviews and Survey B allow the construction of the European Policy-Making Model. Indeed, through the use of both the matrix and the model, a substantive theory is constructed that illustrates convergence and harmonisation procedures in the EU. They also link the categories used in Survey A, the interviews and Survey B. Ultimately, a substantive theory of European integration is illustrated that has aspects of formal theories and meta (see the substantive theory pp24-28).

The Interview Results

In general, the interviews indicated agreement on a number of points. The Third Life Assurance Directive was unanimously perceived as a means of providing the environment that would allow mutual recognition to be achieved; it was also acknowledged that many influences went into the drafting of a directive. Since 1988 interaction between industries and the Commission has become more apparent at the EU level. The representative of DG XV considered that consistent contact with the life insurance industry was imperative in respect of legislative input.

Under the emerged categories of *Understanding, Negotiation, Interaction, Difference* and *Compromise* a general understanding of *European integration* is identified. The interview coding illustrates the parts individual institutions play in the formulation and construction of legislation. Primarily, the coding categories were continually re-affirmed as the main processes of *European integration*. In each interview section the categories merged under the core category of European integration and supported a process of an interaction between self-interest and common interest (this is further illustrated by the Policy-Making Model and Survey B p21).

Axial Coding

Axial coding involves bringing the analysis together, creating a whole. It indicates the overall system of which the categories created through open coding are part. In this study axial coding is illustrated through the interviews and subsequent European Policy-Making Model[3] (see Figure Three).

---

[3] There are two general directions that could be taken regarding policy-making procedures identified on the model. These are indicated by arrows A and B; process A considers that demands are formulated through the national legislature prior to formulation at the EU level; whereas route B illustrates demand formulation being compromised at the EU level prior to the involvement of the national legislature. Route A is a stronger intergovernmental approach whereas route B illustrates more of a neo-functional process. Of course, the situation is not as clear-cut as depicted and elements of both routes were in use but in general the interviews emphasised route B.

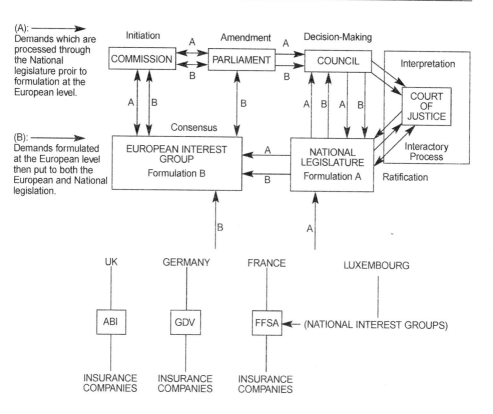

Figure Three: The European Policy-Making Model

An application of axial coding in this research was identified in the following way. The *causal conditions* and *phenomenon* were indicated as membership of the EU and the on going evolution of the SEM. The *context* the possible transfer of sovereignty in terms of the policy-making process and market control. The *intervening conditions* the necessities of harmonisation and the implications this has for integration; such is illustrated through the compromises made by Member States in respect of regulatory environments. This portrays the need for *action/interaction* between Member States and the European policy-making institutions in terms of the evolutionary changes taking place, i.e. the need to harmonise and create a SEM and the goal oriented interaction of creating legislation as close to one's own as possible. Finally, the consequences were identified as the creation of the SEM through harmonisation and a shift toward closer union and greater European integration.

Axial coding allows a more focused means of discovering and relating categories and the research uses Corbin and Strauss' axial coding as a guide into which emerge the specific categories to the study i.e. those categories outlined above. During the interviews further sub-categories emerged which provided the basis of the European Policy-Making Model and added to the substantive theory (see Corbin and Strauss, 1990; pp 96-97).

Selective Coding

"Selective coding is the process by which all categories are unified around a core category" (Corbin and Strauss, 1990; p 15). The core category in this study is European integration. The SEM in life insurance and regulatory environments incorporate " . . . other categories and stand in relationship to the core category as conditions, action/interactional strategies, or consequences" (ibid). The selection of data and the creation of sub-categories have been processed with the core category in mind. Sub-categories that emerged during the initial stages of the research include *liberal, prescribed* and *state-controlled* and those that emerged through the interviews, *understanding, negotiation, interaction, difference* and *compromise.*   "The core category represents the central phenomenon of the study. It is identified by asking questions like: what is the main analytical idea presented in this research? What does all the action/interaction seem to be about?" (ibid). The answers to which in this context are the integration processes at work in the EU. How Member States' action/interaction create the SEM and how this adds impetus to European integration. These areas are identified and unified through axial coding. "During axial coding, one begins to notice certain patterns . . . and a certain amount of integration naturally occurs" (ibid p 130). Indeed, a network of conceptual relationships already exists. Of course, the network may be unclear but these can be refined during selective coding. "It is very important to identify these patterns and to group the data accordingly, because this is what gives the theory specificity" (ibid). To clarify connections in the network grounded theory uses " . . . a combination of inductive and deductive thinking, in which we move between asking questions, generating hypotheses, and making comparisons" (ibid, p 131). Selective coding integrates the research, it puts the story straight, provides analysis, identifies the core category and illustrates how major categories relate, both to it and to each other. This can be further developed through understanding *process.*

Process: Self-Interest & Common Interest

Process is also built into the theory. "Process analysis can mean breaking a phenomenon down into stages, phases, or steps. Process may also denote purposeful action/interaction that is not necessarily progressive, but changes in response to prevailing conditions" (Corbin and Strauss, 1990; p 10). Consequently, when the life insurance industry and EU policy-making institutions are analysed, processes and action/interaction are identified through interest groups. And the changes and compromises made by interest groups and sectors are interpreted in relation to the changes the SEM has brought and is bringing about.

The analysis identified process in the formulation of Member State regulatory structures because of their membership of the EU and the need to harmonise different regulatory environments. This would create the need for sub-categories; and the research sought to identify why and how these changes would take place. Subsequently, the European Policy-Making Model (Figure Three) was constructed through semi-formal interviews, observations and a further survey 'Survey B' (see Data Collection Scheme Table One and p24). The surveys assisted in generating substantive theory. Survey A was used as secondary analysis in relation to the open coding of Member State regulatory structures. Indeed, it added to and verified the initial open coding. "Comparative analysis requires secondary analysis when populations from several different studies are compared, such as different nations or factories" (Glaser and Strauss, 1967; p 188). In the same way Survey B is used as secondary analysis with regard to the European Policy-Making Model.

There is some debate about why companies join interest groups. Olson (1971) considered that collective goods were logically irrelevant to companies when they joined interest groups. He claimed that selective incentives were the reasons for group formation, not some collective good. However, Grant and Marsh (1977) and Marsh (1978) provided evidence that companies do not simply join interest groups for services or selective incentives, but for the collective good as well. Moe (1980) builds on Olson's model and replaces it with a " . . . broader perspective that links the decision to join with varying individual perceptions and indicates that members may join for political reasons if they think their contributions 'make a difference' in providing some of the collective good" (p 6). Furthermore, Moe (1980) argued that the pluralist model focused too much on the political elements of the debate, whereas Olson (1971) over emphasises the non-political.

To substantiate reasons for interest group use, 'Survey B' investigated the extent to which the UK insurance industry used interest groups at the national and European level. For this survey 70 questionnaires were sent out and 36 (50%) were returned. When asked if they used a European interest group in their participation of the formulation of the Third Life Assurance Directive 81.4% said no. Yet, 81.5% considered that they used a national interest group in most cases, the ABI and BIIC. The BIIC negotiates on behalf of the ABI at the EU level and represents the views of the ABI's membership. The link between the European and national interest groups was further substantiated by questions three and four, 85.2% did not directly use European interest groups at all and 74.0% contended that they didn't even subscribe to one, whereas, 100.0% of respondents subscribed to a national interest group. Even when their European interests were threatened 77.7% of companies did not directly approach European institutions whereas 51.8% would approach their national government. However, 59.2% would usually use interest groups to lobby on their behalf at the European level and 89.9% at the national level. When asked if they prefer to use interest groups at the European level to enable European-wide industry compromises 81.5% of respondents rejected this idea. However, 85.2% used interest groups at the national level because this enabled nation-wide compromise. In general, national interest groups are members of European interest groups, which pursue national sector/industry compromises at the EU level; it is through this process that European-wide compromises are reached and the importance of European interest groups emphasised. Indeed, the survey results indicate that UK insurance companies do not lobby on their own behalf in the EU, in the main, they rely on interest groups.

The evidence suggests that the EU insurance industry relies on European-wide interest groups and the notion of collective action. Survey A identified the self-interest of individual companies in relation to the best regulatory environment for their company. Through the national interest group these individual preferences are compromised to form a common interest. Indeed, a common good is sought and reached at the national level. Finally, the national preferences are compromised at the EU level. Through interaction with a supranational institution, sub-national interests identify a common interest.

The Substantive Theory
The substantive theory is built through coding, categorisation and process. The matrices provide the basis of the substantive theory in that they acknowledge that separate Member States pursue different regulatory regimes. This sets up the problem of understanding how compromise is reached. The interviews, observations and Survey B further construct the substantive theory. A substantive

theory has implications for the formal theories of intergovernmentalism and neo-functionalism (in terms of formal spillover, supranationality and interest group utilisation) as well as meta/substantive theories.

The substantive theory was constructed through an inductive/deductive process. The inductive element encompassed the creation of a matrix through coding and categorisation. This was added to and verified by Survey A, this led to a number of deductions. Through axial coding elements of the research were linked around the core category and through selective coding the European Policy-Making Model was formulated. In practical terms, this meant that through the construction of the matrix, we discover that different Member States pursue different concepts of a regulatory environment. This leads the paper to the question whether the Member States compromise their differences and if they do how this is achieved? The interviews provided an understanding of how compromise is pursued and indicated a generalisation. Indeed, the substantive theory may be summarised in the following way:

(a)   *Sectors/industries (in this context the life insurance industry) negotiate the construction of the SEM and consequently further and intensify European integration. (Neo-functional sub-national interests and intergovernmental national preferences).*

(b)   *Sectors/industries interact in the policy-making process in a number of ways but primarily through the use of national and European interest groups. (Neo-functional supranationalism and sub-national interests).*

(c)   *Each Member State's sector/industry compromises it's own interest at the EU level (this is achieved through national interest groups, e.g. ABI, and European interest groups, e.g. CEA).(Neo-functional sub-national interests).*

(d)   *Compromise between the EU wide sector/industry and the Commission is reached primarily through interaction and negotiation between European interest groups and European policy-making institutions.(Multi-level governance defined by institutions and historical norms).*

(e)   *Compromise of difference between the EU legislative bodies, national legislatures and interest groups takes place throughout the creation of European legislation. (Multi-level governance).*

(f)   *There is a shift in allegiance (by the national sector industry) from the national legislature to the EU with regard to certain issues. However, the Member States still play an important role in the policy-making process. Indeed, there has been a shift toward joint sovereignty in the creation of EU legislation. Through this process integration is intensified. (Intergovernmentalism, neo-functionalism multi-level governance and historical institutionalism).*

(g)   *Difference is overcome through sub-national interests, supranantionality and spillover. This creates an impetus for further European integration. (Neo-functionalism).*

(h)   *European integration is given impetus by economic industries/sectors pursuing their self-interest in the creation of EU legislation. However, this allows welfare for Europeans in terms of greater prosperity and peaceful co-existence. Through understanding difference European integration is intensified. (Intergovernmentalism, neo-functionalism, multi-level governance and historical institutionalism.)*

The substantive theory takes into consideration the special nature of life insurance and other financial services products. Indeed, this work considers that products such as life insurance and pensions are closely linked to individual cultures. "Differences in the way distinct countries subjectively value insurance products have not come into being by chance. They have evolved out of historically developed differences in values between one national society and another" (Hofstede, 1995; p 423). This situation exists between the separate Member States and relates to financial services products other than insurance. From this starting point, it is assumed that a study of the life insurance industry can allow generalisations about the EU regarding other financial services industries and sectors. Through spillover generalisation is identifiable with regard to insurance and financial services legislation. The work recognises the limitations of such a generalisation and does so with these in mind. In this context, there is *fit, comprehendibility, generalisation* and *control.*[4]

As noted above, grounded theory uses diagrams make the substantive theory explicit, in this study the following diagrams have been used:
Regulatory/Legislation Environment (Table 2)
Regulation Scale (Table 3)
Life Insurance Regulation Matrix One (Figure 1)
Life Insurance Regulation Matrix Two (Figure 2)
The European Policy-making Model (Figure 3)
The Spillover Model (Figures 4 and 5).

---

[4] Spillover is observed in terms of the need for further legislation in the European life insurance industry and the industries (non-life insurance, banking and pensions) and sectors (capital) related to it. It is suggested that EMU will intensify the need for harmonisation in these areas and it is in this context that intergovernmental and neo-functional processes can be observed. In institutional terms spillover can be seen the creation of the Treaties and agreements that further integration, i.e. ECSC, EEC, Enlargement, Direct Elections, SEA, SEM, EMU. While in functional terms spillover may be observed in two areas (a) in one industry (the insurance industry) vertical spillover; (b) spillover from industry to industry (from insurance to banking) horizontal spillover.

Institutional Spillover	FUNCTIONAL SPILLOVER VERTICAL SPILLOVER WITHIN SAME INDUSTRY	
EPU?		
EMU 1999	X5 ←——————→ X8	
	X4 ←—————— X7	
SEM 1992	X3	
SEA/QMV 1987		
Direct Elections 1979	X2 ←——— X6 X1	
EEC/Euratom 1957		
ECSC 1951		
	INSURANCE	

Figure Four: Neo-Functional Spillover. Vertical Spillover (Within Same Industry)

X1. Re-insurance Directive
X2. Co-insurance Directive
X3. First Life Insurance Directive. 79/267/EEC
X4. Second Life Insurance Directive. 90/ 619/EEC
X5. Third Life Insurance Directive. 92/96/EEC
X6. First Non-Life Insurance Directive. 73/239/EEC
X7. Second Non-Life Insurance Directive. 88/357/EEC
X8. Third Non-Life Insurance Directive. 92/49/EEC

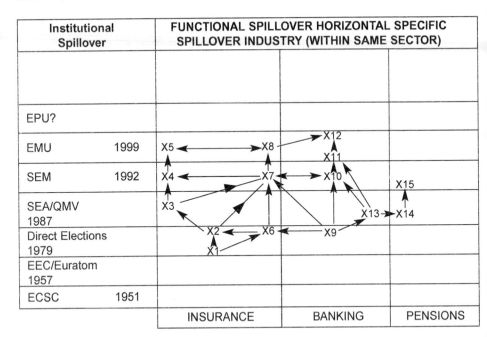

Institutional Spillover		FUNCTIONAL SPILLOVER HORIZONTAL SPECIFIC SPILLOVER INDUSTRY (WITHIN SAME SECTOR)		
EPU?				
EMU	1999			
SEM	1992			
SEA/QMV 1987				
Direct Elections 1979				
EEC/Euratom 1957				
ECSC	1951			
		INSURANCE	BANKING	PENSIONS

Figure Five: Horizontal Specific Spillover (Industry to Industry Within the Same Sector)

X1. Re-insurance Directive 64/225/EEC
X2. Co-insurance Directive 78/473/EEC
X3. First Life Insurance Directive. 79/267/EEC
X4. Second Life Insurance Directive. 90/ 619/EEC
X5. Third Life Insurance Directive. 92/96/EEC
X6. First Non-Life Insurance Directive. 73/239/EEC
X7. Second Non-Life Insurance Directive. 88/357/EEC
X8. Third Non-Life Insurance Directive. 92/49/EEC
X9. First Banking Directive. 77/780/EEC
X10. Second Banking Directive. 89/646/EEC
X11. Capital Adequacy Directive. 93/6/EEC
X12. Solvency Ration Directive. 94/7/EEC
X13. Accounts Directive for Banks and Other Credit Institutions. 86/635/EEC
X14. Directive Concerning Equal Treatment for Men and Women in Occupational Social Security Schemes. 86/378/EEC
X15. Directive Concerning the Rights of Residence for Self-Employed Persons Who have Ceased Occupational Activity. 90/365/EEC

Conclusion

This study illustrates grounded theory techniques in the following ways:

Firstly, a comparative analysis through the open coding of individual Member States' life insurance legislation and regulatory regimes; formulates a regulatory/legislation table and a regulation matrix. Further coding through a survey of Member State insurance industries refined and verified the matrix. These procedures illustrated the need for a further survey, which allowed data saturation and an in-depth understanding of the phenomenon. Indeed, this investigation raised questions regarding how legislative differences between Member States may be resolved.

Secondly, through axial coding and an interview programme, process was identified and illustrated through the European Policy-Making Model (Figure Three). Process is made explicit through Survey B and the analysis relating to self and common interest. Indeed the analysis identifies an interaction between self and common interest that propels integration forward.

Thirdly, the selective coding process is illustrated by the matrix and the model fitting together around the core category of European integration through the creation of the SEM and European Union. Axial coding draws all parts of the analysis together: it is the pivot or the axis of theory building. This is illustrated through the European Policy-Making Model. Finally, a generalisation is made regarding this understanding of legislation formulation, which indicates both neo-functionalism and intergovernmentalism in the process of European integration. Overall, the research identifies the interactive and hierarchical aspects that exist between formal and substantive theory. In this context, substantive theory is formulated in relation to the formal theories of intergovernmentalism, neo-functionalism, multi-level governance and historical institutionalism. However, the article recognises that the latter two theories could be seen as either meta or substantive theory in relation to the former. Through grounded theory techniques, a substantive theory is constructed which furthers our understanding of European integration theory and the evolving European Union.

References

Bulmer, S. Burch, M. Carter, C. Hogwood, P. and Scott, A. (2001) *European Policy-Making Under Devolution: Britains New Multi-Level Governance.* European Policy Research Unit (EPRU) Paper No 1/01 Department of Government Manchester University.

Bulmer, S. (1997) *New Institutionalism, the Single Market and EU Governance.* Arena Working Paper WP 97/25

Bulmer, S. (1994) The Governance of the European Union: A New Institutionalist Approach. *Journal of Public Policy* Vol 13 No 4 pp 351-380

Camerra-Rowe, P. (1996) *Firms and Collective Representation in the European Union.* The American Political Science Meeting. The San Francisco Hilton and Towers. Aug 29-Sept 1. The American Political Science Association.

Carlson, R.E. (1984). *The Nurses Guide to Better Communication.* Glenview III; Scott Forseman and Co.

Charmaz, K. (1983). *The Grounded Theory Method: An Explication and Interpretation. In Contemporary Field Research. A Collection of Readings,* Editor R. M. Emerson. University of California L. A.

Coen, D. (1998) European Business Interest and the Nation State: Large Firm Lobbying in the European Union and Member State. *Journal of Public Policy,* 18 1, pp 75-100.

Coen, D. (1997) The Evolution of the Large Firm as a Political Actor in the European Union. *Journal of European Public Policy.* 4:1 March pp 91-108.

Coleman, W. and Grant, W. (1988) The Organisational Cohesion and Political Access of Business: a Study of Comprehensive Associations. *European Journal of Political Research.* 16: pp 467-487.

Comite Europeen Des Assurances CEA (1990) Note on the Proposal for a Third Life Directive (October).

Comite Europeen Des Assurances CEA *Doc.* MC 093 09/90.

Comite Europeen Des Assurances CEA *Position Papers* (various).

Comite Europeen Des Assurances CEA (no date) *Codification of European Insurance Directives.*

Comite Europeen Des Assurances (1994) *CEA INFO.* November and December.

Commission of the European Community (1985)*White Paper on Completing the Internal Market.* Brussels.

Commission Report (1992) *Completing the Internal Market.* European Commission Jan.

Cottingham, J. and Hussey, R. (1996). *A Grounded Theory Study of Related Party Transactions.* Conference paper Portsmouth University.

Corbin, J. and Strauss, A. (1990). Grounded Theory Research: Procedures Canons and Evaluative Criteria. *Qualitative Sociology.* Vol 13 pp 3-21.

Financial Times Management Report. (1992) *Insurance in the EC and Switzerland Structure and development towards harmonisation.*

Garrett, G. and Tsebelis, G. 1996 An institutional critique of Intergovernmentalism. *International Organization* 50, 2, Spring, pp 269-99.

George, S. (1994) *Supranational Actors and Domestic Politics: Integration Theory Reconsidered in the Light of the Single European Act and Maastricht.* Sheffield Papers in International Studies No 22. (University of Sheffield).

George, S. (1995) *Politics and Policy of the European Community.* Oxford: Oxford University Press.

Glaser, B. (1978). *Advances in the Methodology of Grounded Theory. Theoretical Sensitivity.* University of California, San Francisco.

Glaser, B. (1992). *Emergence vs Forcing. Basics of Grounded Theory Analysis.* Sociology Press: Mill Valley CA.

Glaser, B. and Strauss. A. (1967). *The Discovery of Grounded Theory.* New York: Aldine de Gruyter.

Glaser, D. (1995) *Normative Theory* in Marsh, D. and Stoker, G. Theory and Methods in Political Science. Macmillan Press.

Grant, W. (1995) *Pressure Groups, Politics and Democracy in Britain.* London P. Allen.

Grant, W. (1990) *Organised Interests and the European Community.* Paper presented to Fetrinelli Foundation; Cortona Italy May.

Grant, W. and Marsh, D. (1977) *The Confederation of British Industry.* Hodder and Stoughton London.

Greenwood, J. (1997) *Representing Interests in The European Union.* The European Union Series. Macmillan London.

Greenwood, J. (1995) (ed) *European Casebook on Business Alliances. European Casebook Series on Management.* Prentice Hall International (UK).

Greenwood, J and Cram, L. (1996) European Level Business Collective Action: The Study Agenda Ahead. *Journal of Common Market Studies.* Vol 34, No 3.

Greenwood, J. Grote, J. and Ronit, R. (Eds) (1992) *Organized Interests and the European Community.* Sage.

Guba, E. G. and Lincoln, Y. S. (1994) *Competing Paradigms in Qualitative Research* in Denzin, N. and Lincoln, Y. S. Handbook of Qualitative Research. pp 105-117. Sage: Thousand Oaks.

Guy Peters, B. (2001) *Institutional Theory in Political Science. The New Institutionalism.* Continuum London and New York.

Haas, E. B. (1958). *The Uniting of Europe.* Stanford University Press

Haas, E. B. (1964) *Beyond the Nation State. Functionalism and International Organization.* Stanford University Press.

Haas, E. B. (1964a) *Technocracy, Pluralism and the New Europe* in A New Europe. Ed Graubard S. R. Boston.

Heathcote, N. (1966) The Crisis of European Supranationality. *Journal of Common Market Studies.* Vol 5 December no 2 pp 140-171.

Hix, S. (1994) The Study of the European Community: The Challenge to Comparative Politics. *West European Politics,* Vol 17 No 1 pp 1-30.

Hix, S. (1999) *The Political System of the European Union.* Macmillan. London.

Hofstede, G. (1995) Insurance as a Product of National Values. *The Geneva Papers on Risk and Insurance,* 20 No 77 October pp 423-429.

Howell, K. E. (2000) *Discovering the Limits of European Integration:* applying Grounded Theory. Nova Science New York.

Howell K. E. (1999) European Union Governance: Sub-National Interests, Supranantionality and the Life Insurance Industry. *Current Politics and Economics of Europe.* Vol 9 No 1 pp 95-115. Nova Science New York.

Keohane, R. and Hoffman, S. (1990) *Community Politics and Institutional Change in The Dynamics of European Integration* (ed) Wallace, W. The Royal Institute of International Affairs. Pinter. London and New York.

Keohane, R. and Hoffman, S. (1991) *Institutional Change in Europe in the 1980s in The New European Community: Decision Making and Institutional Change.* Westview.

Lindberg, L. (1963) *The Political Dynamics of European Economic Integration.* Stanford University Press.

Loheac, F. (1991) Deregulation of Financial Services and Liberalization of International Trade in Services. *The Geneva Papers on Risk and Insurance Issues and Practice.* No 61 October pp 406-413.

Luchner, J. E. (1992) *International Relations Theory and European Integration: the Political Economy of the European Monetary System and the SEA.* Ph.D Thesis. The Pennsylvania State University.

Majone, G. (1990) *Introduction in Deregulation or Re-regulation? Regulatory Reform in Europe and the United States.* pp 1-2.

Majone, G. (1994) The Rise of the Regulatory State in Europe *in West European Politics.* Special Issue on *The State in Western Europe: Retreat or Redefinition?* Eds Muller, W. C. and Wright, V. vol 17 No 3 July. Frank Cass London.

Majone, G. (1996) *A European Regulatory State?* in European Union Power and Policy-Making (ed) Richardson J. J. Routledge London and New York.

March, J. G. and Olsen, J. P. (1998) *The Institutional Dynamics of International Political Orders.* Arena Working Papers WP 98/5.

Marks, G. (1993) *Structural Policy and Multilevel Governance in The State of the European Community. The Maastricht Debate and Beyond Vol 2* (eds) Calfruny, A. W. and Rosenthal, G. G. Lynne Rienner. Longman.

Marks, G., Hooghe, L. and Blank, K. (1995) *European Integration and the State.* European University Institute Working Paper No 95/7.

Marks, G., Scharpf, F. W., Schmitter, P. C. and Streeck, W. (eds) (1996)

Governance in the European Union. Sage London.

Marks, G., Hooghe, L. and Blank, K. (1996a) European Integration from the 1980s: State-Centric v. Multi-level Governance. *Journal of Common Market Studies* Vol 34, No 3.

Marsh, D. (1978) More on Joining Interest Groups. *British Journal of Political Science.* Vol 8 pp 380-384.

McLaughlin, A. M. (1995) *Automobiles: Dynamic Organisations in Turbulent Times?* in Greenwood, J. *European Casebook on Business Alliances.* pp 172-183. Prentice Hall International UK.

McLaughlin. A. M. and Greenwood, J. (1995) The Management of Interest Representation in the European Union. *Journal of Common Market Studies* Vol 33, No 1. March pp 143-146.

McLaughlin, A. M. *et al.* (1993) Corporate Lobbying in the European Community. *Journal of Common Market Studies* Vol 31 No 2. June. pp 192-213.

Moe, T. M. (1980) *The Organisation of Interests.* University of Chicago Press. Chicago and London.

Munich Re, (1988). *A Series of Notes on Insurance in the EC.*

Nye, J. S. (1971) *Comparing Common Markets: A Revised Neo-Functionalist Model in Regional Integration: Theory and Research.* Lindberg, L. & Scheigold, S. A. (eds) Cambridge Mass: Harvard University Press.

Olson, M. (1971) *The Logic of Collective Action: Public Goods and the Theory of Groups.* Harvard University Press.

Oyen, E. (Ed) (1977). *Comparative Methodology Theory and Practice in International Social Research.* CA: Sage.

Pierson, P. (1996) The Path to European Integration: A Historical Institutionalist Analysis. *Comparative Political Studies.* Vol. 29 No. 2 April pp 123-163. Sage.

Salafatinos, C. (1996) *Applying Grounded Theory in Management Accounting Research: A Case Study of ABC Implementation.* Conference paper Portsmouth University: UK.

Sandholtz, W. (1994) Choosing Union: Monetary Politics and Maastricht in Neilsen, B. F. and Stubb, A. C-G. (Eds) *The European Union. Readings on the Theory and Practice of European Integration.* Lynne Rienner London.

Sandholtz, W. and Zysman, J. (1989) 1992: Recasting the European bargain. *World Politics* Vol 42, pp 95-129.

Sandholtz, S. and Stone Sweet, A. (1998) *European Integration and Supranational Governance.* Oxford University Press UK.

Scheingold, S. (1971). *Domestic and International Consequences of Regional Integration* in Lindberg, L. & Scheigold, S. A. (eds) *Regional Integration:* Theory and Research. Cambridge Mass: Harvard University Press.

Swiss Re, (UK). (1989). *Sigma* no 2.

Swiss Re, (UK). (1990). *Sigma* no 1.

Swiss Re, (UK). (1990). *Sigma* no 4.

Swiss Re, (UK). (1991). *Sigma* no 2.

Swiss Re, (UK). (1992). *Sigma* no 1.

Strauss, A. (1987). *Qualitative Analysis for Social Scientist.* New York: Cambridge University Press.

Strauss, A and Corbin, J. (1990). *Basics of Qualitative Research.* Grounded Theory Procedures and Techniques. CA: Sage.

Strauss, A. & Corbin, J. (1994) *Grounded Theory Methodology An Overview* in Denzin, N. and Lincoln, Y. *Handbook of Qualitative Research* pp 273-285. Sage: Thousand Oaks.

Tranholme-Mikkelson, J. 1991 Neo-functionalism Obstinate v Obsolete. *Millennium* Vol 20 pp 1-22.

Vipond, P. (1995) *European Banking and Insurance: Business Alliances and Corporate Strategy* in *European Casebook on Business Alliances.* (Ed) Greenwood, J. European Casebook Series on Management. Prentice Hall. Hemel Hempstead

Earlybrave Publications

Clinical Effectiveness from Guidelines to Cost Effective Practice	Prof M Deighan/S Hitch	1-900-432-00-5
The Measurement of Meaning: Data Mining and Perspectives on the Trompenaars' Database	Peter Woolliams/ Fons Trompenaars	1-900-432-01-3
The International Debt Problem in Historical Perspective	Derek Aldcroft	1-900-432-02-1
Mixed Good Continua and Public Policy	S Shmanske	1-900-432-03-X
Capital Structure Targeting in European Quoted Firms	Jonathan Tucker	1-900-432-04-8
Piloting Appraisal with Hospital Consultants	Prof Jack Sanger/ Malcolm Stamp	1-900-432-05-6
Determinates of the Marginal Capital Structure Decision	Jonathan Tucker/ Susanne Farrar	1-900-432-06-4
Building Financial Support for SME's in Central & Eastern Europe	Lester Lloyd Reason	1-900-432-07-2
Organisation, Culture & Job Satisfaction	Peter Woolliams/ Tina Mosley	1-900-432-08-0
Towards Culture Free Business Ethics	Peter Woolliams/ Chris Moon	1-900-432-09-9
The Impact of the Macro Economic Environment Upon the European Corporate Capital Structure	Jonathan Tucker	1-900-432-10-2
Managers Exercising Influence: A Case Incident Approach	Chris Swaffin-Smith	1-900-432-11-0
Towards A Unified Model for Small to Medium Enterprise Business Paradigms	Chris Swaffin-Smith/Peter Woolliams/Jim Tomeko	1-900-432-12-9
Supporting Business Professional Students with WEB Technology	Graham Hart/John Webb	1-900-432-13-7
Offensive Marketing A Success in a Small to Medium Sized Manufacturing Enterprise	B Wharton/Alan Jebb/ Chris Swaffin-Smith	1-900-432-14-5
Culture Surveys: Monitoring and Enhancing The Impact of Change Programmes	Chris Swaffin-Smith/Richard Barnes/Marie Christine	1-900-432-15-3
Educational Choice at Post 16: a study into how students determine their preferred post - 16 eductional provider	Jaki Lilly/Andrew Armitage/ Harriet Thomas	1-900-432-16-1
On the Returns of Scores By Professional Golfers	John McCullough	1-900-432-17-X
The Sterling Area in the 1930s: A Unique Monetary Arrangement?	Derek H Aldcroft	1-900-432-18-8
Financial Viability in Small Housing Associations	Paul Saw	1-900-432-19-6
Ask a Stupid Question ...' : Issues in Employee Satisfaction Reseach	Jaki Lilly	1-900-432-20-X
Buyology': Life Beyond the Marketing Mix?	Anthony R Bennett	1-900-432-21-8
An Unravelling of Research Methodology (others, however, might see it differently)	Dr Vernon Trafford	1-900-432-22-6
The Cart before the Horse: Australian Exchange Rate Policy and Economic Reform in the 1980s	Kieron Toner	1-900-432-23-4
Globalisation and the Emergence of New Strategic Directions	Alan Griffiths/Stuart Wall	1-900-432-24-2
The Japanese Employment System: Continuity and Change in a Dynamic Environment	Alan Griffiths/Stuart Wall	1-900-432-25-0

These publications may be purchased directly from the publisher at the following address:

PUBLICATIONS LIMITED

Linda Golding
Earlybrave Publications Ltd
Springfield Lyons House
Chelmsford Business Park
Chelmsford CM2 5TH
United Kingdom

Tel:+44 (0)1245 236584
Fax:+44 (0)1245 236611
Email: lgolding@earlybrave.com

Order on-line at www.earlybrave.com